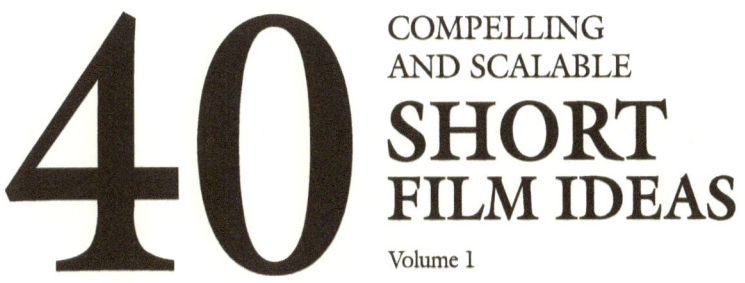

40 COMPELLING AND SCALABLE SHORT FILM IDEAS

Volume 1

by **Chike Camara**

40 COMPELLING AND SCALABLE SHORT FILM IDEAS
by Chike Camara

Second Edition

All rights reserved. No part of this publication may be reproduced, distributed, or transmitted in any form or by any means, including photocopying, recording, or other electronic or mechanical methods, without the prior written permission of the publisher, except in the case of brief quotations embodied in critical reviews and certain other noncommercial uses permitted by copyright law.

Copyright © 2012, 2018 by Akachi LLC

www.theshortfilmidea.com

CONTENTS

Disclaimer	6
Introduction	7
40 Compelling and Scalable Short Film Ideas	8
CASE STUDY: How I Came Up With a Short Film Idea and Screenplay.	15
HOW TO COME UP WITH SHORT IDEAS OF YOUR OWN	19
CONCLUSION	23

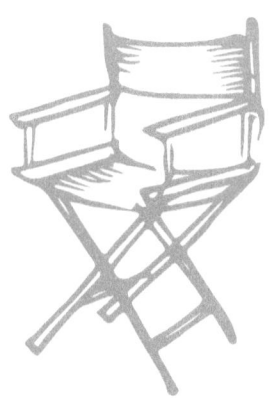

DISCLAIMER

Hi There! Thank you for purchasing this book. We hope that you find these short film ideas useful. We tried really hard to make the ideas scalable and compelling. They are yours to use and change as you wish, however, we ask that if you should make a film based on one of these ideas, simply give us thanks in the credits.

Finally, please note that while these ideas were created by a staff member of Best Screenwriting Books.com and/or Akachi LLC, it is possible that these ideas may be similar to films/ideas that you may have come across at some point. The nature of storytelling is such that no story is truly original.

Know that these ideas have not been plagiarized in any way. Any resemblance to other stories is strictly coincidental. We make no promises that the screenplay that you create will be successful. Need more ideas? We will be rolling out volume 2 by Winter 2012. Keep in mind also that these are short film ideas, not feature film ideas.

Enjoy!

INTRODUCTION

Thank you for purchasing this book. This book of short film ideas was born out of necessity. One day, I was feeling especially creative and felt a strong desire to work on my next film project. I sat in my chair for a long moment trying to come up with an idea. I was drawing a blank. I find coming up with feature film ideas pretty easy, but with a short film… So, I tried everything: recounting a personal experience, recounting someone else's personal experience, putting a new twist on a children's story, on and on and on… Nothing.

Then I imagined what it must be like for other screenwriters who were trying to write their next screenplay. I looked on the internet for short film ideas and it seemed everybody was looking for them yet nobody had any answers. So I decided to help by coming up with a bunch short film ideas. But first, I'd have to come up with one for myself and then figure out how I can reproduce the process. Then I remembered a key rule when it comes to writing: "Know Your Ending First".

I went back to one of my life experiences story and remembered how it didn't end so well. There was a clean, solid ending. So now that I had my ending, I knew where I had to go from the beginning. The idea was easy to formulate after that…

Following are 40 short film ideas that I believe are compelling, varied, and scalable. And the price is very reasonable Please visit our website at http://www.bestscreenwritingbooks.com if you'd like to get in touch with us. Take care and happy writing…

Chike Camara
New York City 5/2012

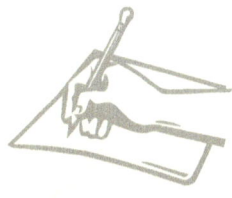

40 (COMPELLING AND SCALABLE) **SHORT FILM IDEAS**

1. An 11 year old high school senior (a genius) has a difficult relationship with her underachieving 18 year old sister who happens to be a senior at the same school. But when a short, sudden illness takes the 11 year old's life, it forces her sister to reexamine her priorities. In a final, touching homage to her sister at her grave, she reveals that she got straight A's since her sister had died and just found out that she was accepted into a prestigious university.

2. After being assigned to head an Italian crime family, a sensitive wise guy complains to a cohort about running two families: the crime family and his own which includes a new bride, a newborn, and a dog named Gambino. When his wife demands he devote his time to her, the kid, and the dog, and after some soul searching, he does what he knows he has to do...get rid of one problem to solve the other.

3. In flashback, we recount the last 2 hours of a heroin-addicted teen's life as various people who were close to her read from a devastating open letter in her diary that she wrote just before her last shot of heroine.

4. After arriving to class early, an overweight student takes the chance to express his love to his beautiful cheerleader classmate who has also arrived early; Upon hearing him out, she begins to berate him to no end with insults and laughter... And as students enter, the boy wets himself, then passes out, hitting his head on the floor. Her shock and resulting silence in the room as blood crawls from under his head make for a tragic and sad little story.

5. An old woman (70s), recently diagnosed with Alzheimer's and dressed in a wedding dress, insists that her visiting father (90s) take her to the church and walk her down the aisle to hand her off to her handsome marine husband. Unable to convince her that she was married years ago and that her husband died 10 years ago, he gives in and gives her her wish. We watch as they make their way slowly down the stairs, then slowly through the front door and into a big, old 1960's Mercedes Benz. The car rolls slowly away as the sun is setting.

6. An amusing little film about a life-like teenage robot who has trouble trying to figure out a girl's "features" such as flirting, not really saying what she means, kissing, emotions, etc. Frustrated, she leaves as he repeatedly proclaims "I love you. I love you. I love you. I love you."

7. After both serving 17 years in jail for two-separate crimes committed in two different parts of town, a 34 year-old man and his 55 year-old father are reunited through a "bringing families together" organization. They struggle to accept each other until the pain of an incident during the son's childhood is confronted, understood and accepted when both seek out and connect with their now-married mother/wife.

8. A character study on a handsome superhero who while caught up in his own narcissism, makes it easy for the villain to press the red button that will end the world!

9. After a district attorney and his activist wife are robbed at gun point inside their home, they visit the robber in prison to get answers. What results is a very unlikely friendship between the two men after the robber is released.

10. Believing that he's her soul mate, a woman falls for her organ donor; problem is, he's married. Whether they end up together is a matter of life and death...in an ironic and tragic twist, his wife dies.

11. A wannabe teenage singer rehearses daily to be on "American Idol"; Her dreams are crushed when the day before her audition, she "auditions" in front of a tough preliminary panel of judges: her mother, her brother and father.

12. As an old man lies dying in his death bed, an odd lot of family members come to terms with his death and in doing so, reveal information that pieces together a horrible family secret... are these people related at all?

13. We recount a relationship backwards, from divorce to pure bliss of that first meeting where the first words uttered between the couple are the exact same ones that are spoken at the end of their relationship.

14. December 20, 2012, the day before the Mayans predict the world would end, a teenager convinced of impending doom, reveals comes out of the closet to his stunned and disappointed minister parents. On December 22, 2012, he commits suicide.

15. A parable about a 20-something investment banker who leaves work one day in search of the Secret of Life and returns home to his suspicious live-in girlfriend that same evening 60 years older and wiser. According to her, "This just isn't going to work out". Or is it? The question is, would she like to know the secret as well? Does she bail on the relationship or does curiosity get the best of her? To the degree she loves him determines her decision.

16. Intrigued by the mysterious man she's trying to help, a widowed suicide hotline operator goes against code and calls the man. After a brief courtship and subsequent affair she learns that not even love can delay the inevitable.

17. For her initiation, a new angel is assigned the strange task of getting a Jewish young man and Muslim young woman to fall in love on December 25. Do they fall in love? Or is it possible that not even an Angel can affect the barriers to unconditional love that humans put up?

18. On their 21st birthday, two now-fatherless sisters try to come to terms with their mother leaving them in the care of their drunk father at a young age so that she can start a new family. Ironically, they find her drunk and alone. The healing begins when one a step sister they've never met stops by the house to check in on their mother.

19. A MAN gets more than he bargained for when a prostitute he ordered to his hotel room turned out to be his daughter; the ensuing family therapy session between husband, wife and daughter is hilarious, yet poignant.

20. After their mother reveals years of their father cheating on her, two teenage sisters go to their adulterous father's job and "break up" with him.

21. After being robbed at gunpoint, a young man turns investigator, trying to track down the man who robbed him; His only clue: a pair of vintage sneakers… Meanwhile, after being filled with guilt, the robber attempts to track down the young man to return his wallet and cash. The tables are turned when they meet; robber becomes victim, victim becomes robber.

22. Inspired by Saint Augustine, a young man investigates what it takes to become a saint. Shortly thereafter, he decides to let go of his past and devotes his life to becoming a saint until a disagreement with one of his former buddies escalates into a brutal fight over money. His quest to become a saint is short-lived.

23. At the urging of his wife a retired, paunchy superhero with an ill-fitting costume, goes on a quest to find the villain-turned-hero who forced him into retirement; little does he know, finding him was all part of the villain's plan; what will a final man-to-man battle with the use of no weapons and no powers reveal? "Good always beats evil."

24. Near the end of writing her novel, a woman goes on an unusual quest to find the word she's looking for.

25. A woman on a bus overhears an emotional phone conversation and in a tragic twist of fate experiences what the phone conversation was about: the sudden tragic death of her mother.

26. A man reunites with his teacher after 40 years when the teacher's daughter reaches out to him after reading his memoir about a fateful event that changed his life forever: at age 6, he had a seizure while crossing the street and was nearly run over by a speeding car; the teacher saved his life. Emotions flow as they enjoy a cup of coffee together in the commercial building that was once the school they attended. ...And the teacher's daughter is kind of cute too...

27. A man with short-term memory loss finds HIMSELF on an online dating website and falls in love AGAIN - with the woman he broke off his engagement to. She plays along, hoping he'd forgotten that he didn't really love her.

28. A teenager steals stories from a "player" in his English Literature class and uses them to seduce the girl of his dreams...who happens to be the player's favorite ex-girlfriend.

29. 1946. A young boy loses his dog-shaped balloon. To appease him, his mother makes a cursory drive around the neighborhood looking for it. They don't find it.; Sometime later, the mother takes him to a doctor in another town and complains that he hasn't said a word in two months what can she do? "Give it time" the doctor advises.; On a cloudy windy day, just as the sun has set, the mother's military husband returns home bringing her joy and a cute little dog he found while making his way home.

30. 1955. A new groom, listening to a baseball game, tells his new bride he's going to the market; He never returns. A year later, the woman sits alone knitting while pregnant. Listening to a baseball game. Another man arrives home from work and greets her (and her tummy) lovingly... Fast forward to the present: an old man watches his grandson playing little league baseball. He's sitting next to an old woman who is watching her grandson play baseball. They strike up a conversation about nothing much. The weather.

Their love for the town... But it's what is not said between them that reveals the truth...that they were the newlyweds in 1955 whose lives were changed when he walked out on her, and they both know it.

31. A gothic character study about a woman who is bitten by a vampire during a one night stand, and then must decide whether to bite her 5 year old son or spare him. Does the remnants of love preclude her from harming her son? Or does the natural urge to suck his blood overtake her? How strong is love? ...Early in the morning, she decides to run out of her house into the sunlight and crumbles into pieces in the yard for all to see.

32. Refusing to accept his son's condition, a retired superhero tries to teach his blind son a super power: how to "see". He gives up, frustrated...until his powerless son reveals a special power that trumps all super powers...the power of unconditional love...

33. A handsome yet unsatisfied man who could have almost any woman he wants, decides to conduct an experiment after reading his horoscope: date one woman from each sign of the zodiac to find his true love. After choosing none of them, he finds love in an ironic way: he meets a woman who was abandoned then adopted at a young age...no record of her birth exists.

34. A girl who loses her virginity gets really creative when goes home to break the news to her psychic mother...

35. After his 9 year-old son is caught stealing from a convenience store, a former superhero decides it's time to have "the talk"...

36. Think raucous house party, someone keeps playing pranks at first, innocent ones on individuals. Then on groups of people. Then the stakes are raised when someone is seriously hurt. Then someone dies, then a few more people until... Three people are left. Who's the killer?

37. After a misdiagnosis of cancer and impending death, a young man without any musical background struggles to complete a song his late-father was trying to compose; but he manages to complete it and the resulting success of the song garners him newfound success. On his follow-up visit, the doctor informs him he does not have cancer, he has a harmless condition called hyperplasia.

38. A fictitious experiment where high-ranking government officials question a group of men and women about ordinary things in their lives. But something's odd: The men talk about things that the women would normally discuss, and vice versa. Guys talk about the new necklace they've bought, fashion, their children, their weight...Women talk about their new video game systems, upgrading their computer, the hot female roommates upstairs... After an assessment and confirmation that things are progressing nicely, a grand experimental project is revealed by one of the officials.

39. A dramatic comedy about a girl with disabilities who challenges her little brother to do certain tasks (chores, games, etc.) without the aid of certain abilities he has (by not using his legs, or his arms, or his sight etc.) and takes for granted. By the end, he is in tears and expresses deeply the love he has for his sister.

40. The ultra conservative parents of a young married woman complain about the new neighbourhood the couple and their baby has moved into. The bride has doubts. The groom loves the place. They get into an argument and don't talk for a day. Fast forward to the next morning. The bride makes her way into the back yard. "I could love this place. I guess. Sweetie?" The groom joins her. They make up... Then they notice the back gate open. A neighbour who's raking his yard says that the police were looking around their back yard for a gun. The bride gives her husband "that look." Later, with baby in tow, as they walk to the car they notice a gun on top of their SUV. The groom's final line is priceless.

CASE STUDY
How I Came Up With a Short Film Idea and Screenplay

I recently wrote a short screenplay entitled "Delilah" about an 18 year old prostitute who, after having a heart-felt dinner with a high school friend, is forced to choose between continuing her prostitution or getting her life together before something bad happens to her. It has been produced as part of a series of short films that together will make up my first feature film. For that reason, I cannot share the screenplay. However, this story is focused on the process I used to come up with the story. I am very happy with its outcome.

Let me tell you the process I went through in writing the short film. The idea for the short film came from an interview I saw on a morning talk show in the United States. A 14 year old prostitute was discussing what "tricking" was like for her. The thing that struck me was how unemotional the prostitute was. She seemed to have this notion that money was what was important. She also seemed to accept the fact that her life might end tragically. However, as the host began to discuss more of the young lady's past, the young lady's hard shell began to soften a bit. All the signs of denial were there, and I thought: wow, this is interesting. So I decided to do a story about a character with that temperament....

So, okay, I have a young prostitute who is in denial about the danger of what she's doing and who's focused on "making money." The first thing that I start thinking about is what's my ending? What happens to the young prostitute? I thought: she gets raped. Now, that ends up changing a little as I worked through the screenplay, but I have a good solid ending where something happens to the main character.

Now the next question is, because most short films have an ironic or twist ending, what can I do to the rest of the script to make the sort of ending I have be of that type? (Note: a short screenplay doesn't have to have a twist or clever ending; it's a question I like to ask because I happen to like those types of stories. Let's face it, the short screenplays and films that win awards are typically ones that surprise the reader or viewer).

Okay, so this young prostitute gets raped. That's my ending as of now. Thinking back to the talk show, I remember certain questions the host asked seemed to affect the young girl in subtle ways. So I thought I'd bring in another character to be her "interviewer." Someone who could bring out some of Delilah's sensitivities and insecurities. How could I do that? What I ended up doing was having her talk with an old high school buddy who she'd lost contact with. They could be on a bus, at dinner - wherever... I decided to go with Delilah and her old high school friend having dinner.

Now, in film, it's always advisable to think of ways in which you can create conflict. Opposition causes conflict. By it's very nature, put a priest and an atheist convict in the same room! So, sure, I could have her talking to a female high school mate just talking over a meal, but how can I create a sense of conflict? More importantly how is this conflict at odds with the end of the end of the story?

First, I decided that the friend should be a guy. Getting deeper into "oppositions", I decided to make him be of a different race than Delilah. Further, I decided that it will be established that he asked her out in high school, and that she rejected him because he was a "geeky nerd type." But I wanted to give the sense that they were friendly to each other on some level in high school. So there's that opposition: geeky nerd vs. popular pretty girl. There's also a tension created by his attraction to her and her apparent lack of attraction to him. I also wanted this character to have some sort of profession or social life that was in opposition some way to Delilah's. So, in keeping with the geeky nerd idea, I had him be a student enrolled at an Ivy League college (after all, they are both late teens).

It's always good to ask questions that take you deeper into character. So I said, okay, what's his major? And, since he acts as "interviewer" to Delilah, I decided on psychology.

Okay so we have an Ivy League college student and a prostitute who went to high school together talking at dinner. Interesting. So I decided to simply have them "catch up" on life after high school. This talk would eventually turn into a bit of a psychiatrist session and conflict with Delilah in some way... Also, I'm always thinking of how I can humanize characters and also add to the overall story. So I decided to establish that Delilah had plans to go into the Marines after high school. This sort of makes human and helps the audience to connect with her.

So I had my story: a young prostitute and an Ivy League student who are former high school mates have dinner and discuss their lives. In the end, the young prostitute is raped.

The story is missing something. I needed a bridge between the dinner and Delilah getting raped. Since I wanted this to be more of a character study I decided to make what they were discussing be at odds with what happens to her at the end. That way, I could have a bit of a plot and also reveal the character I'd like to show by having them discuss something that makes her uncomfortable.

So how could I begin the story? For a short film (or any film for that matter), you want to start with a bang. After all, they're sitting at dinner having a conversation! Could be boring right? Not if what they're talking about is interesting though. So I decided to have them sort of sit in silence for a bit, being uncomfortable. Then I had her friend ask her a question that most inquisitive men probably wonder about: "So what's it like to have sex with all those different guys." So that sorta breaks the ice. So he begins to ask her more and more serious questions until he gets her to soften up a bit and she begins to crack. He ends by making her aware of the real danger of doing what she does and warns her something could happen to her.

So the only way to make that work is to have her do something against (or in opposition to) that warning. So, after their dinner, I have them say their goodbyes and leave each other. What she does is, she ignores his warning and goes to work - turning tricks. After work, I wrote that she gets on the train and sits. She begins to think, pondering what happened at dinner. Then we see two rough looking thugs at the other end of the train car staring at her... I left it at that because I didn't think that we needed to see the rape to understand that that's what will happen to her. I wanted to leave it open-ended. I thought really hard, though, about whether the audience would "get" the ending. It's very important to consider if the audience will comprehend what you've written.

See? I took something I saw from an interview and turned that into a short film idea... If you see something interesting (an event or an interaction between people), build around that and develop a short film!

HOW TO COME UP WITH SHORT IDEAS OF YOUR OWN

Short Film Case Studies
If you don't know how to come up with short film ideas of your own, following are a few case studies that will help point you in the right direction. You can also find more on my website https://www.theshortfilmidea.com.

SHORT FILM IDEA – CASE STUDY #1

So, following are a couple case studies on how to come up with short film ideas so that you'll be armed with enough knowledge to create your own short films. As the saying goes "Give a man a fish, he'll eat for a day; TEACH a man to fish, he'll eat for life." So, over the next several days, we'll show you by example how to come up with short film ideas.

The following short film idea question was posed on Yahoo! Answers. Let's see if we can help him or her...

"I need to create a short film for a year 10 assignment, i want to get an A and my teacher expects a lot from me i need it to be amazing! any ideas?"

This is a typical question; it's VERY general. Where do we start? Luckily the subject line read HORROR SHORT FILM IDEAS....

A good place to start is to see if you can find a pretty decent definition of what a horror film is (i.e. Wikipedia). Believe it or not, this can provide you with a bit of clarity of what you're trying to accomplish.

Another step would be to think of some of your favorite horror films. What did you like about them? What made them scary? What made them dumb (if you like dumb horror movies)?

Also, the simplest way to approach this is to take a major 5 to ten minute turning point in a horror film that you really like and write a screenplay based on that sequence. Use just that sequence as a guide. Sequences are usually 10-15 mins. DO NOT PLAGIARIZE. Change up the characters and add a couple twists of your own. How could this sequence be done differently?

Finally, for fun, here's an idea...

As a favor, young but argumentative newlyweds agree to watch their 10-year-old niece while her parents catch a movie and dinner together. Little do the newlyweds know that their niece isn't quite the angel everyone thinks yet the end result of her actions is that it brings the newlyweds closer together.

That's what the short film is about. Now a few questions to ask so that I can really nail down the story could be:

1. What happens at the end to the niece and newlyweds.
In fact, that should be the first question I ask, because if I know this, everything else can sort of be built towards that end. It's a horror movie, so what qualities does the story need to have for it to be deemed a "horror film?"

Let's look at the following Wikipedia entry for "horror film":

A horror film is a film that seeks to elicit a physiological reaction, such as an elevated heartbeat, through the use of fear and shocking one's audiences. Initially often inspired by literature from authors like Edgar Allan Poe, Bram Stoker, and Mary Shelley, horror has existed as a film genre for more than one century. The macabre and the supernatural are frequent themes. Horror may also overlap with the fantasy, supernatural fiction, and thriller genres.

Horror films often aim to evoke viewers' nightmares, fears, revulsions and terror of the unknown. Plots within the horror genre often involve the intrusion of an evil force, event, or personage into the everyday world. Prevalent elements include ghosts, extraterrestrials, vampires, werewolves, demons, satanism, evil clowns, gore, torture, vicious animals, evil witches, monsters, zombies, cannibalism, psychopaths, natural or man-made disasters, sharks and serial killers.

I see terms like "supernatural", "ghosts", "vampires", and "vicious animals." So, I know that one of the main characters has to do something out of the ordinary to elicit emotions such as fear and horror. It's clear from the idea above that the niece will be the character that'll put the "horror" in our short film.

2. Who causes the horror?
So, I've established the niece as the one causing the horror, bringing about the fear.

So far, I haven't asked questions such as why a character is this or that. I'm just trying to establish the story – the idea, and then I can get into all of the subplot and themes. Plot, subplot, and theme is beyond the scope of this blog post, but I'll do another series of post on theme, structure and short film plot.

3. What special ability does the horror-inducing character have? This is key; once I know this, I can create scenarios where that ability will cause the newlyweds (and hopefully audience) to be in fear.

Let me take a quick stab (pun intended) at these three questions.

1. The newlyweds survive the horror. The niece returns back to "normal." Ok great, we have an ending. But this is not enough for us to go on though. If you've read my Short Film Structure Secrets book, then you'd know that this ending is a surface one, it doesn't provide specific actions of the characters that symbolize the end of their problem. But we do have an ending towards which we can guide this ship of a short film.

2. The niece causes the horror.

3. So I'll just establish that the niece has the special ability to assume someone else's voice – to imitate anything. How'd I come up with that idea? Well, I thought about some of my own fears, and one of my fears is hearing voices of deceased people, or God forbid my own voice being reflected back at me from some hidden place. Then I thought, this would be good to play off the fact that the newlyweds are argumentative. This power or ability the niece has can be used to accentuate that. Perhaps the niece doesn't want to be "baby sat" or she's resentful that her parents didn't take her with them.

Ok, so now I can re-write my logline a bit so that I can have a clearer short film idea. Here's the original one:

As a favor, young but argumentative newlyweds agree to watch their 10-year-old niece while her parents catch a movie and dinner together. Little do the newlyweds know that their niece isn't quite the angel everyone thinks yet the end result of her actions is that it brings the newlyweds closer together.

And here's it again but tweaked for clarity:

Young but argumentative newlyweds agree to watch their 10-year-old niece while her parents catch a movie and dinner together. Little do the newlyweds know is that their niece isn't quite the angel everyone thinks. When the niece uses her special ability to imitate people and animals to try to scare the newlyweds off, all hell breaks loose until the newlyweds figure out the nieces "off switch". In the end, the ordeal brings the newlyweds closer together and the niece turns back to normal.

So, there you have it! Obviously, some blanks need to be filled in, but we have a short horror film idea.

SHORT FILM IDEA - CASE STUDY #2

Recently, we read on the internet the following question regarding short film ideas. It's a great example of how to take something from real life and generate a short film idea:

I need some ideas for new short films, I am making an application for OCHSA. Please nothing super crazy, I don't have many things to edit with, my laptop isn't very good. I am trying to do more silent films too. Thanks!

OUR ANSWER: A cool idea may be doing a short film about your experience in applying for OCHSA… But substitute the process for something possibly absurd, like a young person filling out an application and applying for something from his/her parents. Make the whole process like an actual application process…. This would make both a comical and cute story that an audience would connect to. Hope this helps!

This is something the writer can tap into quickly as he/she is applying for something right now. Why not take that process and make a short film out of it?

SHORT FILM IDEA – CASE STUDY #3

Another short film idea request from the internet.

Ideas for short iMovie film? :)?

My friends and I (we're only in the 8th grade :P) are playing around with iMovie. We made the start of a scary movie, where somebody gets pulled under a bed by a monster.

Now we really want to continue it, but we have no idea what to film next. Suggestions?

(and keep in mind we don't have any fancy effects).

OUR ANSWER: Hi there. Well in film, the audience secretly wants to know why…. Did you setup the fact that there was something strange about the bed in the beginning? Anyway, next could be a discovery phases where a parent or big brother or sister comes into the room and can't find that somebody; or multiple people come into the room and can't find that person. ALWAYS KNOW YOUR ENDING is what they say in the movie writing business. So, do you know how it will end? If you can concentrate your efforts on figuring out how the story ends, then it will be really easy to finish your film.

Let's say that in the end, everything is as it was the moment before the person was sucked under the bed by a monster. Well, a good thing to do is to show the difference between choices. For example, if that person chooses to be mean to someone (while talking on the phone or whatever), then they got sucked under the bed. Or, if that person chose to be supportive, then they don't get sucked under the bed. BUT you have to establish in the beginning that if a person makes a wrong choice, something bad will happen.

Anyway, let's say you want to start with that person getting sucked under the bed from the beginning. Then it'd be a good idea to spend the rest of your film showing why and how this happened. Don't need special effects, just action.

One idea that has come to mind is this: what if the person who got sucked under the bed was caused by a fear by his or her little sister or brother who sleeps in that room. The little sister or brother of the person sucked under the bed is really, really afraid at night and has a strong fear that there is a monster under there. Let's say it's a little sister. And let's say the person who got sucked under the bed is an older brother. The little sister's fear is so strong that it causes her older brother to get sucked under the bed. Why? Because the older brother does the one thing that causes the fear for the little sister in the first place. For example, if the little sister thinks that the monster only comes at night when a secret word is said (let's use, for example, the word "Brussel sprout"), then the monster will get that person.

And let's say that this little girl is so afraid that one night, her mother asks her older brother to switch rooms a couple days. And let's say that, the older brother is up late, doing something he's not supposed to do (like being on the laptop at night on a school night), and while instant messaging someone, he says out loud "…I hate brussel sprouts" – then he gets sucked under the bed!

So, now, were back to the present. How does he get out from under the bed? Well, let's say we know that the ending is that he returns to where he was right before being sucked under the bed. The only way that he can get out is if his little sister faces her fear and says the secret word in her bedroom, when it gets dark. Her mom and dad help her to face her fear by talking about it and getting her to say the word in her room. When she does, her brother appears.

Something like that. Needs to be developed a little more, but hopefully this has helped point you in the right direction!

Thanks for reading.

CONCLUSION

So there you have it. A variety of 40 short film ideas for you to customize to create your next short film. I've also given you a process by which you can quickly come up with your own ideas. Just remember that there is a story in anything; you just have to add conflict and point the story towards a clear end. If you'd like to learn and understand some of the most common plot structures for short films, consider reading my book "SHORT FILM STRUCTURE: Secrets".

PLEASE BE SURE TO RATE THIS BOOK on the site where you purchased it. Rating books helps authors a lot!

www.ingramcontent.com/pod-product-compliance
Lightning Source LLC
Chambersburg PA
CBHW031512210526
45463CB00008B/3218